52 Ways to Motivate Yourself: A One Year Journey for Living a Positive Life in a Complicated World

by

John Bentley

INTRODUCTION

My daughter passed away in Dec 2010. Her death was unimaginably impactful and emotionally painful. Over the next five years I turned into a workaholic, gained weight, my emotions were in turmoil, and I lost my way in the painful grief of losing my child. I lost my way to living a meaningful life. A friend who was concerned about my negative downward spiral recommended I collect motivational and inspiring quotes – pieces of wisdom that became iconic over the ages – and use them as a foundation to shift my mental and emotional attitude.

This quote collection allowed me to focus, to take back and rebuild my fragile and emotional psyche, enabled me to create and develop small goals and then larger goals, to take the action steps, and – finally – to get back to living a life I loved. I offer these same life-inspiring quotes (52, one weekly, for a calendar year) to you, with tips, reflections, and a small set of questions enabling you to empower yourself to think about what negative ideas and emotions are holding you back and what positive goal setting, actions, and thoughts you can strive for to improve your mental and emotional health. These motivational quotes help you move past self-imposed limitations, and while your life situation may not be the same as mine, use the empowering exercises to help you gain more from your life within a year.

When the weight of the world gets you down, it's easy to give up, scrap an idea, or fail to see a greater opportunity when it presents itself. During these moments a little motivation can do wonders to help you stay positive and move forward.

This book comprises 52 weekly pages highlighting thoughts and ways to motivate yourself. Each of the 52 weekly ways consists of...

- ... a motivational quote to encourage you,
- ... a few words to positively shift your thinking,
- ... three recommendations to get you going, and
- ... three self-reflection questions for better action.

While you may read the book cover-to-cover, I suggest you start and finish each week with one quote along with the reflections that speak to your specific situation. You may jot notes in the pages under each self-reflection question or use your own note book or separate journal into which you write your reflections.

Don't feel you have to do each week sequentially – it is OK to skip around to weeks that may seem more relevant to your life at the time based on the quote's focus. Live a little and be daring – go against the flow if you want to break out of the rut!

Once you have completed the 52 weeks of motivation and inspiration, you will complete a one-year journey of building the momentum to create and sustain a positive life and attitude in spite of tough times that may have come your way.

After all, life is what you make of it. Use these bits of wisdom to lift you up – even when you don't feel like it – you *will* come out on top!

Normally book sections start on the right-hand side of the book – on the odd pages. This book is a little different in that you can read the quotes and reflections on the left-hand side, then review the reflection questions on the right; this enables you stay on the same idea on facing pages. The author hopes this serves you well in your reading, thinking, and reflection exercises.

WEEK 1

BLESSED ARE THE
FLEXIBLE, FOR THEY
SHALL NOT BE BENT
OUT OF SHAPE.

ANONYMOUS

It's far less difficult to get angry or fly off the handle when you manage your emotions as difficulties occur in your life. Learn to effectively lead yourself during times of stress is critical.

Do your best to not let stress engulf you. It's easy to let negative feelings pile up until they all pour out at once. When you can easily adjust to changes or difficult situations, you'll lead a much happier, healthier, successful life.

- Learn to let trivial things go.
- Don't hold your feelings inside.
- There's no such thing as perfect.

Self-Reflection Questions:

1. How can I become more aware of and manage my feelings?

2. How do I behave when things don't go the way I planned?

3. How will I remove myself from negative situations when necessary?

At the end of this week of reflection:

1. This week's quote and tips were relevant in my life because:

2. My reflections resulted in me understanding:

3. The benefits I will receive by applying my understanding are:

WEEK 2

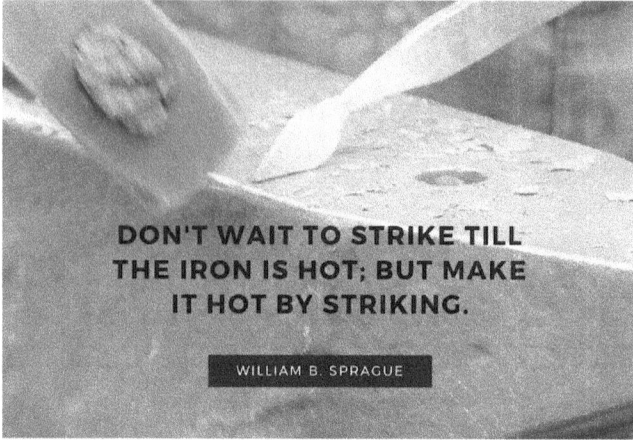

DON'T WAIT TO STRIKE TILL THE IRON IS HOT; BUT MAKE IT HOT BY STRIKING.

WILLIAM B. SPRAGUE

Success will not always come looking for you. You must be proactive and find opportunities to attain the success you desire. Take the initiative to do more than what is expected of you each day.

Be excellent in your work so you will be noticed. Then, when the opportunity presents itself, take the steps you need to make the most of it.

- Be proactive.
- Always take the initiative.
- Do what you can to make opportunities happen.

Self-Reflection Questions:

1. How can I become more aware of the opportunities around me?

2. What will I do to create new opportunities?

3. What additional tasks will I do to continue to improve?

At the end of this week of reflection:

- This last week's quote and tips were relevant in my life because:

- My reflections last week resulted in me understanding:

- The benefits I will receive by applying my understanding are:

WEEK 3

I DO NOT TRY TO DANCE BETTER THAN ANYONE ELSE. I ONLY TRY TO DANCE BETTER THAN MYSELF.

MIKHAIL BARYSHNIKOV

Do you compare yourself to others? If you do, I encourage you to stop now. The only person you need to compete with is *you!*

If you're constantly trying to keep up with others, you'll never feel like you've fully succeeded. Strive to better yourself first and success will surely follow.

- Determine what you'd like to improve about yourself.
- Identify the necessary steps to become a better you.
- Now, work on those things one-by-one.

Self-Reflection Questions:

1. Do I know what I want out of life, or am I just following everyone else's lead?

2. How will I take the time to access, accept, and act on my designed natural talents?

3. How does comparing myself to others negatively impact me and others?

At the end of this week of reflection:

- This last week's quote and tips were relevant in my life because:

- My reflections last week resulted in me understanding:

- The benefits I will receive by applying my understanding are:

WEEK 4

**BELIEVE IT IS POSSIBLE TO SOLVE YOUR PROBLEM.
TREMENDOUS THINGS HAPPEN TO THE BELIEVER.
SO, BELIEVE THE ANSWER WILL COME. IT WILL.**

NORMAN VINCENT PEALE

Believing in yourself is not always easy during difficult times, but knowing you are making the best possible choice in the moment is the only way to find your answers. Believing in yourself builds confidence, motivation, and the willingness to learn.

The possibility to solve your problems always exist. Will it take time – sure – just keep believing and keep working toward your main goal; the answers will be there in the end.

- Look at the problem from all angles.
- Believe in yourself and your ability to solve the problem.
- Allow yourself the patience to find the answers.

Self-Reflection Questions:

1. What will I do to have a better perspective of the problems I face?

2. How far does my self-confidence take me in solving the issue?

3. How will I patiently work hard to find the answers I need?

At the end of this week of reflection:

- This last week's quote and tips were relevant in my life because:

- My reflections last week resulted in me understanding:

- The benefits I will receive by applying my understanding are:

WEEK 5

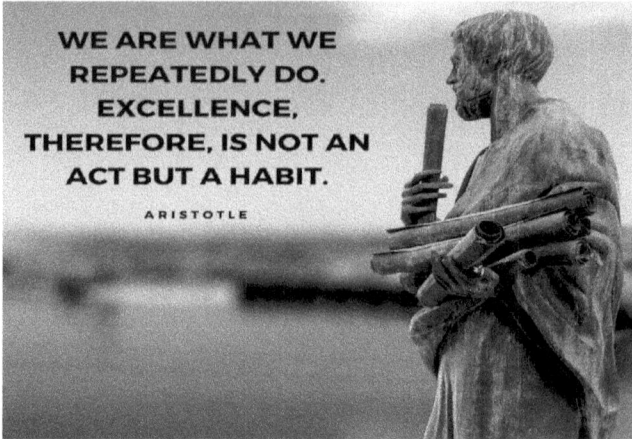

WE ARE WHAT WE REPEATEDLY DO. EXCELLENCE, THEREFORE, IS NOT AN ACT BUT A HABIT.

ARISTOTLE

You are often known by what you do more so than by what you say. If you are consistent in your actions, especially in your work ethic, people will take notice.

Don't do a good job, do a great job! Your consistent behavior in your job will translate to excellence, and that is what your employer and life will reward.

- Be consistent.
- Do a great job.
- Do more than expected.

Self-Reflection Questions:

1. What must I do to be more consistent in my actions?

2. How can I perform my best work every day?

3. What prevents me from giving my employer my best rather than mediocrity?

At the end of this week of reflection:

- This last week's quote and tips were relevant in my life because:

- My reflections last week resulted in me understanding:

- The benefits I will receive by applying my understanding are:

WEEK 6

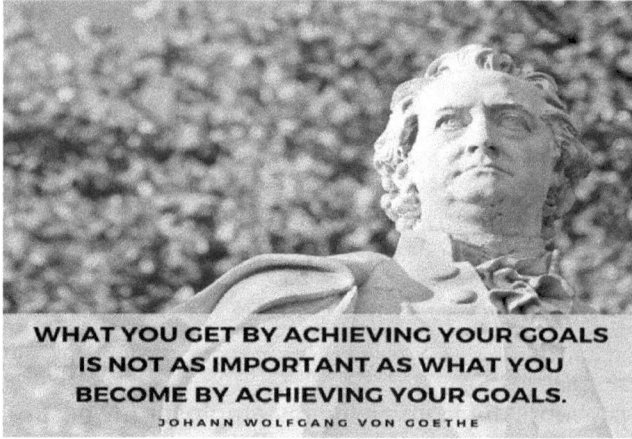

WHAT YOU GET BY ACHIEVING YOUR GOALS
IS NOT AS IMPORTANT AS WHAT YOU
BECOME BY ACHIEVING YOUR GOALS.

JOHANN WOLFGANG VON GOETHE

Do not get so focused on achieving your goals that you do not enjoy the process or the journey along the way. Yes, it's true that you set goals in hopes that you will achieve them; however, there's more to life than merely meeting a goal.

You should try to become a better person while striving to meet and exceed the goals you have set for yourself.

- Set attainable goals.
- Work toward achieving those goals.
- Take time to learn about yourself as you work to attain your goals.

Self-Reflection Questions:

1. How can I measure my growth as I work toward goals?

2. Determine if your goals are attainable vs. too difficult to reach?

3. What prevents me from following through on my goals to reach them?

At the end of this week of reflection:

- This last week's quote and tips were relevant in my life because:

- My reflections last week resulted in me understanding:

- The benefits I will receive by applying my understanding are:

WEEK 7

KEEP AWAY FROM PEOPLE WHO TRY TO BELITTLE
YOUR AMBITIONS. SMALL PEOPLE ALWAYS DO THAT,
BUT THE REALLY GREAT MAKE YOUR FEEL THAT
YOU, TOO, CAN BECOME GREAT.

MARK TWAIN

When you're just starting out, some people may tell you that your dreams are out of reach. Instead of listening to people who don't see your vision or don't believe you can achieve it, find people with a vision of their own.

By spending time with those who have goals for the future, you can learn how to become all you dream to be.

- Stay away from people with no vision.
- Share your vision with those who have their own.
- Reach for your goals despite what small minded people say.

Self-Reflection Questions:

1. What is my vision for the future?

2. Who do I listen to that discourages or encourages me?

3. How have I encouraged others around me with my vision?

At the end of this week of reflection:

- This last week's quote and tips were relevant in my life because:

- My reflections last week resulted in me understanding:

- The benefits I will receive by applying my understanding are:

WEEK 8

TAKE THE FIRST STEP IN FAITH. YOU DON'T HAVE TO SEE THE WHOLE STAIRCASE, JUST TAKE THE FIRST STEP.

DR. MARTIN LUTHER KING JR.

When you are just starting out on our own, taking the first step may be unnerving. Remember you don't have to see the whole future in front of you.

You must take the first step toward your goals whether you can see the next step or not. If you can't take the first step, you will never reach your goals.

- Set goals and know where you want to go.
- Take the first step in faith.
- Keep walking so you can reach your goal.

Self-Reflection Questions:

1. What is the first step I will take to move close to the life I want?

2. What will I do to keep walking toward my goal, even if I don't know the path?

3. Who can support me on my journey to success?

At the end of this week of reflection:

• This last week's quote and tips were relevant in my life because:

• My reflections last week resulted in me understanding:

• The benefits I will receive by applying my understanding are:

WEEK 9

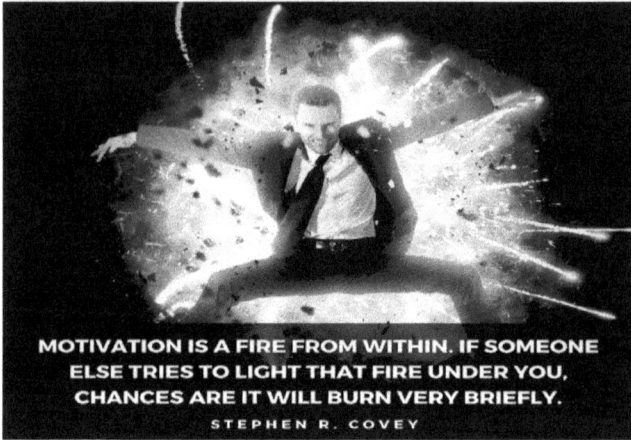

MOTIVATION IS A FIRE FROM WITHIN. IF SOMEONE
ELSE TRIES TO LIGHT THAT FIRE UNDER YOU,
CHANCES ARE IT WILL BURN VERY BRIEFLY.
STEPHEN R. COVEY

Rarely is the case you can catch motivation from others. Others can encourage you to achieve your dreams, but the motivation to succeed must come from within yourself.

You must want something bad enough that you'll do whatever is necessary to succeed. Only you can fan the flames of motivation; no one else can do it for you.

- Decide what you want to achieve.
- Determine how to achieve the goal.
- Don't let others talk you out of it.

Self-Reflection Questions:

1. Why is what I want important enough to keep working and not give up?

2. How will I remain motivated enough to continue despite hardships?

3. What will I do when others suggest I give up?

At the end of this week of reflection:

- This last week's quote and tips were relevant in my life because:

- My reflections last week resulted in me understanding:

- The benefits I will receive by applying my understanding are:

WEEK 10

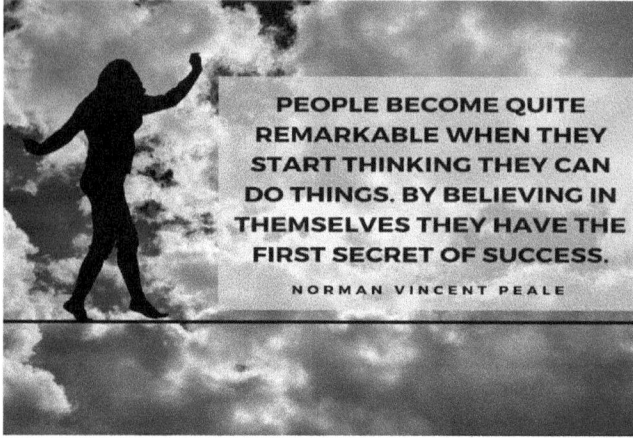

PEOPLE BECOME QUITE REMARKABLE WHEN THEY START THINKING THEY CAN DO THINGS. BY BELIEVING IN THEMSELVES THEY HAVE THE FIRST SECRET OF SUCCESS.

NORMAN VINCENT PEALE

If you don't believe in yourself, no one else will believe in you either. Choose to convince yourself you can do anything you set your mind to doing.

By creating that strong, unwavering belief, you're more than half the way toward achieving any goal you set.

- Know what success you desire.
- Tell yourself that you can do anything you set your mind to.
- Don't let others dissuade you from achieving your goals.

Self-Reflection Questions:

1. Why do I sometimes not believe in myself and give up my goals?

2. When others say I can't succeed, how will I work to remain confident and not give up?

3. Why is determination the key to achieving your desires?

At the end of this week of reflection:

- This last week's quote and tips were relevant in my life because:

- My reflections last week resulted in me understanding:

- The benefits I will receive by applying my understanding are:

WEEK 11

ANYONE CAN DO THINGS WHEN THEY WANT TO DO IT. ALL SUCCESSFUL PEOPLE DO THINGS WHEN THEY DON'T WANT TO DO IT.

DR. PHIL MCGRAW

It's amazing to see how many people are eager to get ahead in life, but they are often unwilling to do what is necessary to be a success. There are going to be things in your journey toward success that you do not want to do.

Take a deep breath, accept what you need to do, and then do it to the best of your ability.

- Take the bad with the good.
- Do the best you can in every task.
- Don't slack off on the grunt work.

Self-Reflection Questions:

1. Name a time I did not work to the best of your ability? Why were you unwilling to give your best?

2. What are some tasks I do not want to do? When I accomplish these tasks how do I feel about myself?

3. What does my work ethic prove to others?

At the end of this week of reflection:

- This last week's quote and tips were relevant in my life because:

- My reflections last week resulted in me understanding:

- The benefits I will receive by applying my understanding are:

WEEK 12

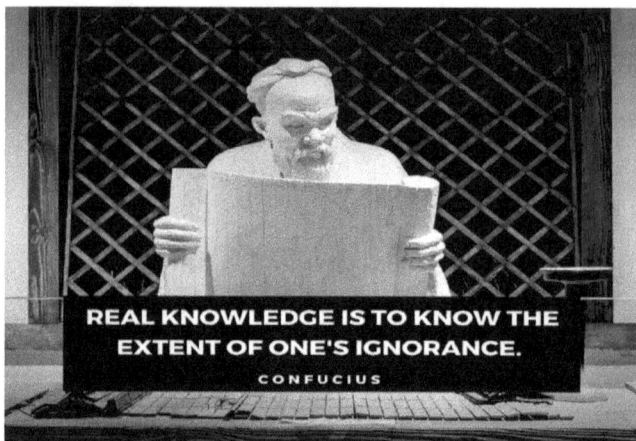

REAL KNOWLEDGE IS TO KNOW THE EXTENT OF ONE'S IGNORANCE.

CONFUCIUS

There are people in this world who will never admit when they are wrong or when they do not fully understand something. To understand anything and reach true wisdom, you must know what areas of your life could use improvement.

Admit you don't know everything. Be willing to constantly learn and improve upon your knowledge and skills.

- Know your strengths.
- Always be open to learning.
- Work to improve your weaknesses.

Self-Reflection Questions:

1. What prevents me from admitting openly when I don't know how to do something?

2. Once I know where I'm in need of development, how willing am I to take the steps necessary to improve?

3. What areas of my life should I focus in gaining more wisdom that will benefit me the most?

At the end of this week of reflection:

- This last week's quote and tips were relevant in my life because:

- My reflections last week resulted in me understanding:

- The benefits I will receive by applying my understanding are:

WEEK 13

WINNERS LOSE MUCH MORE OFTEN THAN LOSERS. SO IF YOU KEEP LOSING BUT YOU'RE STILL TRYING, KEEP IT UP! YOU'RE RIGHT ON TRACK.

MATTHEW KEITH GROVES

When you stop trying to win, your chances of succeeding become less and less. It is like playing the lottery. You can't win if you don't play, and the more you play, the better your odds of winning.

No matter what you do in life, if you practice over and over you'll see improvement.

- Keep trying and think positively.
- Constantly work towards your goal.
- Don't give up.

Self-Reflection Questions:

1. When I start something, and it gets difficult, how can I keep work through the rough times instead of giving up?

2. When was the last time I rewarded myself for little accomplishments on my way to the bigger goal?

3. How can I look for something good in everything situation good or bad?

At the end of this week of reflection:

- This last week's quote and tips were relevant in my life because:

- My reflections last week resulted in me understanding:

- The benefits I will receive by applying my understanding are:

WEEK 14

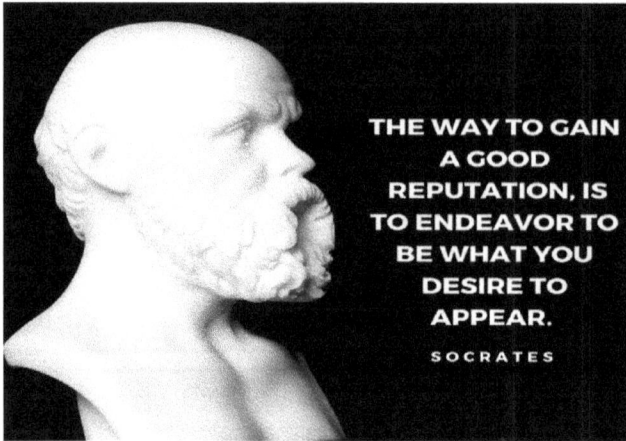

THE WAY TO GAIN A GOOD REPUTATION, IS TO ENDEAVOR TO BE WHAT YOU DESIRE TO APPEAR.

SOCRATES

Society has a way of convincing people they are not as good as the next person. When they cannot measure up to the standards of others, some people will put up a front hoping they will look better in the eyes of others.

Stop trying to conform and start showing your 'true self.' By doing so, you develop your character and a positive reputation with others.

- Take time to remind yourself of your positive traits.
- Determine who you really want to be and show yourself to the world.
- Every day be true to the unique and real you.

Self-Reflection Questions:

1. How am I putting up a front to look good in the eyes of others?

2. What are my positive characteristics? How do these characteristics help me build a positive reputation?

3. As I reflect on myself and my life, what make changes will I make to become more proud of myself?

At the end of this week of reflection:

- This last week's quote and tips were relevant in my life because:

- My reflections last week resulted in me understanding:

- The benefits I will receive by applying my understanding are:

WEEK 15

SEEK THE LOFTY BY READING, HEARING AND SEEING GREAT WORK AT SOME MOMENT EVERY DAY.
THORNTON WILDER

To be a better person and seek the greater things in life, you must first be appreciative of the things already good in your life. Hard as it may be to find, there is a positive to every situation.

You can't have something good without bad and vice versa. Even if it is only one thing, find something positive about yourself every single day.

- When met with negative things, take a minute to search for the upside of the situation.
- Positivism breeds the same.
- Take time to find joy in the little things in life.

Self-Reflection Questions:

1. Am I a negative person? Why am I that way, and how can I change my attitude and thinking?

2. What happens if I see the glass half-full instead of half-empty?

3. How will my positive attitude help someone else through a difficult situation?

At the end of this week of reflection:

- This last week's quote and tips were relevant in my life because:

- My reflections last week resulted in me understanding:

- The benefits I will receive by applying my understanding are:

WEEK 16

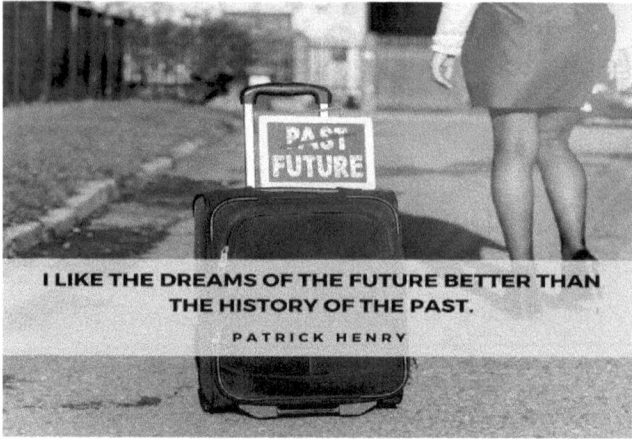

I LIKE THE DREAMS OF THE FUTURE BETTER THAN
THE HISTORY OF THE PAST.

PATRICK HENRY

History is just that – history. You can't change the past, no matter how hard you try. You can make choices and decisions to positively impact your future.

Decide what you want the future to hold instead of living your life in the past. The past will hold you prisoner and detour you from the optimistic things waiting on you in the future.

- History is meant to be read about not lived.
- Start planning for the future.
- See life as exciting and adventurous instead of something you must get through.

Self-Reflection Questions:

1. In what ways am I working to improve myself?

2. How may something in my past be holding me back from living my best life?

3. What choices will I make to determine my new future?

At the end of this week of reflection:

- This last week's quote and tips were relevant in my life because:

- My reflections last week resulted in me understanding:

- The benefits I will receive by applying my understanding are:

WEEK 17

ONLY THOSE WHO DARE TO DREAM CAN
MAKE THEIR DREAMS COME TRUE.
UNKNOWN

If you don't have dreams and aspirations, is life worth living? You cannot expect your wishes to come true unless you make the wish in the first place.

Stop letting life's ups-and-downs keep you from working towards a fulfilled life. If you never take the time to seek the things you want in life, how can those things ever come into being.

- Decide what it is you really want out of life.
- Dare to dream and dream big.
- Set milestones to help you achieve your goals.

Self-Reflection Questions:

1. No matter how big or small, what dreams do I want to achieve?

2. How can I reach my goals one step at a time?

3. What will I do to improve my life on a daily basis?

At the end of this week of reflection:

- This last week's quote and tips were relevant in my life because:

- My reflections last week resulted in me understanding:

- The benefits I will receive by applying my understanding are:

WEEK 18

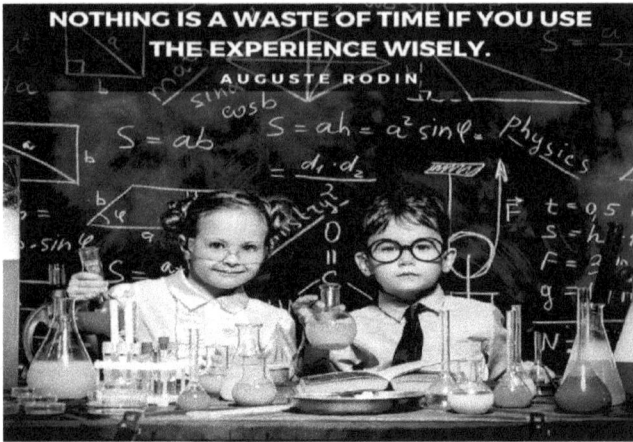

NOTHING IS A WASTE OF TIME IF YOU USE THE EXPERIENCE WISELY.

AUGUSTE RODIN

Everything in life is an experience you can learn from. Be it good or bad, if you take the time to absorb the wisdom which comes from these experiences, you can use them to better yourself and the lives of others.

If you're wrong, there is no shame in admitting the error. You become a stronger person by admitting when you make a mistake instead of placing blame elsewhere or on others.

- Admit when you've made a mistake.
- Learn from your mistakes to avoid making the same one twice.
- Take your experiences and use them for helping others when appropriate.

Self-Reflection Questions:

1. Name a time when you were wrong and was not willing to admit or correct it?

2. What situations got me into trouble and how can I take the steps necessary to avoid them in the future?

3. How can my life experiences help others in some form?

At the end of this week of reflection:

- This last week's quote and tips were relevant in my life because:

- My reflections last week resulted in me understanding:

- The benefits I will receive by applying my understanding are:

WEEK 19

THE VALUE OF LIFE LIES NOT IN THE LENGTH OF DAYS, BUT IN THE USE WE MAKE OF THEM.

MICHEL DE MONTAIGNE

Every day is a gift you've been given to do with as you see fit. Don't waste it. Instead make the most of each and every day.

You don't know just how many days you will end up getting in your life. It would be sad for you to have wasted away such a precious and meaningful gift, just because you didn't make positive use of each day you were given.

- Set goals … know where you want to go.
- Learn the value of life.
- Remind yourself every day that life is a gift.

Self-Reflection Questions:

1. What do I know and value about my life?

2. What one thing am I willing to do to make my time useful? Where can I start?

3. Who can I help that will make my day more meaningful and fulfilling?

At the end of this week of reflection:

- This last week's quote and tips were relevant in my life because:

- My reflections last week resulted in me understanding:

- The benefits I will receive by applying my understanding are:

WEEK 20

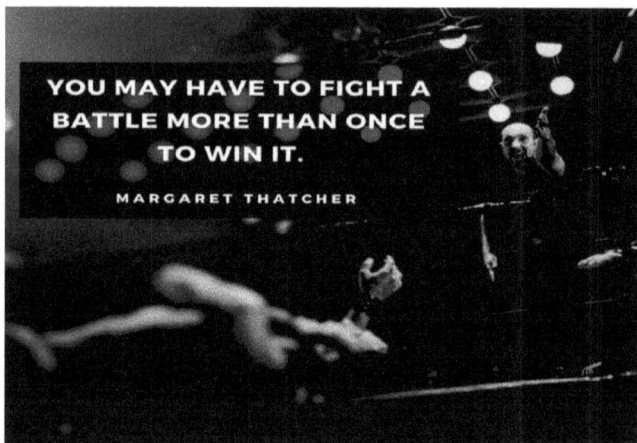

YOU MAY HAVE TO FIGHT A
BATTLE MORE THAN ONCE
TO WIN IT.

MARGARET THATCHER

Patience and perseverance is required to win any battle. Sometimes, the importance of traveling down a path more than once is necessary to gain the knowledge and experience you need to improve your life.

If you think you're going down the same road you've been down before, determine what went wrong the first time so you don't repeat it again.

- Keep pushing forward.
- Learn from your mistakes.
- Keep a positive and patient outlook to continue through your struggles and come out the other side a better person.

Self-Reflection Questions:

1. How do I practice patience to see something through to the end?

2. What lessons have I learned in the past that will help me get through this battle?

3. How do I stay focused and remain willing to keep moving forward even when faced with adversities?

At the end of this week of reflection:

- This last week's quote and tips were relevant in my life because:

- My reflections last week resulted in me understanding:

- The benefits I will receive by applying my understanding are:

WEEK 21

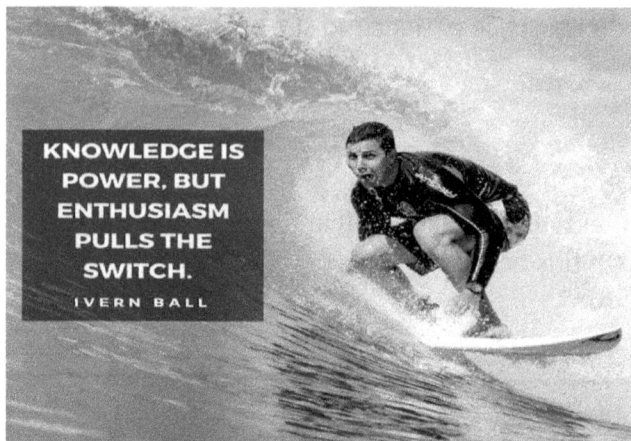

KNOWLEDGE IS
POWER, BUT
ENTHUSIASM
PULLS THE
SWITCH.

IVERN BALL

You can have all the information in the world stored in your mind; however, if you lack the desire or excitement to do anything with that knowledge … it become useless. To be successful at anything you must have an eagerness to apply what you know.

Enthusiasm is like electricity. If you never flip the switch, no one will ever see the glow. You might not use what you know immediately, but never let your knowledge go to waste.

- Learn something new every day.
- Never let knowledge go to waste.
- Do things to keep the enthusiasm going even in difficult times.

Self-Reflection Questions:

1. What can I do to share my passion and knowledge about the activities I enjoy doing?

2. What keeps me motivated to keep chugging along when I really don't want to?

3. How have I applied the information I have learned in my life to make a significant contribution?

At the end of this week of reflection:

- This last week's quote and tips were relevant in my life because:

- My reflections last week resulted in me understanding:

- The benefits I will receive by applying my understanding are:

WEEK 22

Our life will never be perfect, that's a fact. However, if you spend all of your time worrying about what might be coming your way, you will never reap the benefits the world has to offer.

Worry-warts of the world miss out on so many things; if you are a worry-wart you focus all your energy on the things that could happen. Therefore, you miss the good things that have or could have happened.

- Stop worrying so much.
- Take time to enjoy your today because once today is over you can never get it back.
- Focus on the good things in life – no matter how trivial they may seem.

Self-Reflection Questions:

1. How can I record or remember meaningful moments to absorb their impact on me?

2. How can I continue to strive towards my goals, but not be disappointed if I cannot achieve perfection?

3. How am I making the best of each and every day I have been blessed with?

At the end of this week of reflection:

- This last week's quote and tips were relevant in my life because:

- My reflections last week resulted in me understanding:

- The benefits I will receive by applying my understanding are:

WEEK 23

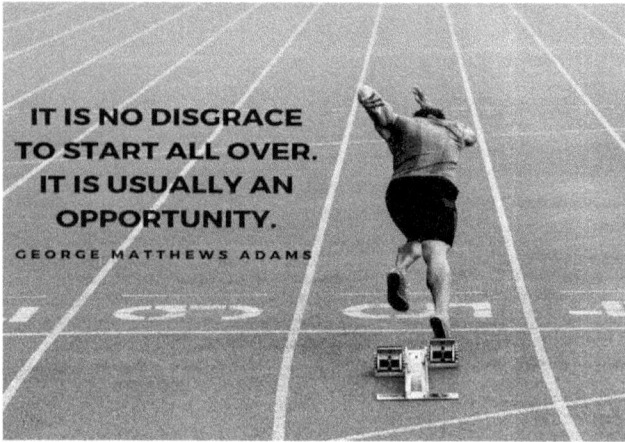

IT IS NO DISGRACE
TO START ALL OVER.
IT IS USUALLY AN
OPPORTUNITY.

GEORGE MATTHEWS ADAMS

People see themselves as failures when something they are working on goes wrong. For this reason, they scrap the whole idea.

What do you think would happen if you started the process over again, knowing what you didn't know the first time around? Greatness just might be achieved. Go for it, instead of allowing humiliation to take over your thoughts.

- Don't be afraid to make mistakes.
- Don't wait for opportunities to come your way, create your own!
- Keep your eyes open for opportunities can come about in the oddest of places.

Self-Reflection Questions:

1. Do I truly understand the power of the lesson learned?

2. No matter how bad I feel, can I promise to not give up without first trying again?

3. Am I comfortable enough in my own skin that I can start over without feeling humiliated or shameful?

At the end of this week of reflection:

- This last week's quote and tips were relevant in my life because:

- My reflections last week resulted in me understanding:

- The benefits I will receive by applying my understanding are:

WEEK 24

You hold yourself back for a multitude of reasons. Wondering if you will end up with joy or disaster can stop you.

You should never be afraid to try! Shooting for the moon is a learning process that can always bring something good into your life.

- Think about some things you'd like to try in your life.
- Determine what's holding you back from attempting them.
- Allow yourself the strength to push forward.

Self-Reflection Questions:

1. What do I really want to accomplish in my life?

2. Why am I afraid to try new things? What's stopping me?

3. Why is important I accept small successes on the way toward my ultimate goals?

At the end of this week of reflection:

- This last week's quote and tips were relevant in my life because:

- My reflections last week resulted in me understanding:

- The benefits I will receive by applying my understanding are:

WEEK 25

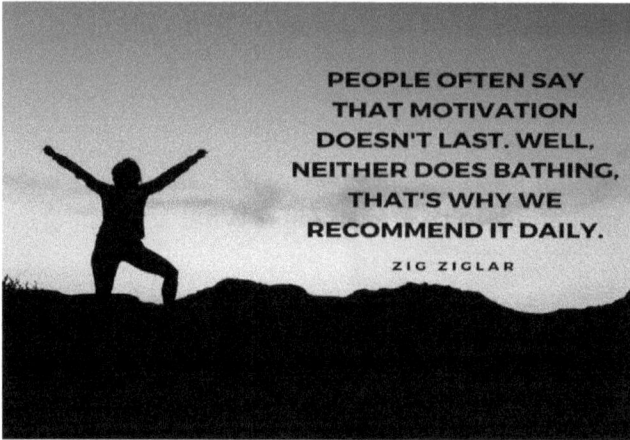

PEOPLE OFTEN SAY
THAT MOTIVATION
DOESN'T LAST. WELL,
NEITHER DOES BATHING,
THAT'S WHY WE
RECOMMEND IT DAILY.

ZIG ZIGLAR

Motivation enables you to strive for a better life and fulfill your dreams. On a daily basis you need motivation.

Motivation can come from many sources, but the best source is from within oneself. When you can motivate yourself every day, the sky is your limit.

- Search within yourself to find the things that motivate you.
- Use these motivations daily to achieve your goals.
- Don't be afraid to change what motivates you.

Self-Reflection Questions:

1. What motivates me?

2. How are my motivation sources helping or hindering me?

3. How am I striving to use these motivations to enhance my life on a daily basis?

At the end of this week of reflection:

- This last week's quote and tips were relevant in my life because:

- My reflections last week resulted in me understanding:

- The benefits I will receive by applying my understanding are:

WEEK 26

OUR DEEPEST FEAR IS NOT THAT WE ARE INADEQUATE. OUR DEEPEST FEAR IS THAT WE ARE POWERFUL BEYOND MEASURE. IT IS OUR LIGHT, NOT OUR DARKNESS, THAT MOST FRIGHTENS US.

MARIANNE WILLIAMSON

From the wealthy to the poor, from the highly educated to the uneducated, you may have felt, at one time or another, that you should step away, and allow the flow to go outside your realm of comfort.

The power to shine has been given to you! You should never allow yourself, for any reason, to live dismally. Bring forth all of yourself so others may see you for the wonderful person you are.

- Reach within yourself to find the reasons you hide in the shadows.
- Access and accept your greatness.
- Let your gifts shine so you can benefit yourself and others.

Self-Reflection Questions:

1. What do I know about that I can do better than others? Am I a subject matter expert that I can share my experience and wisdom with others?

2. How can I share my talents and knowledge to benefit others?

3. What causes me to become withdrawn because I may be better at something than others.

At the end of this week of reflection:

- This last week's quote and tips were relevant in my life because:

- My reflections last week resulted in me understanding:

- The benefits I will receive by applying my understanding are:

WEEK 27

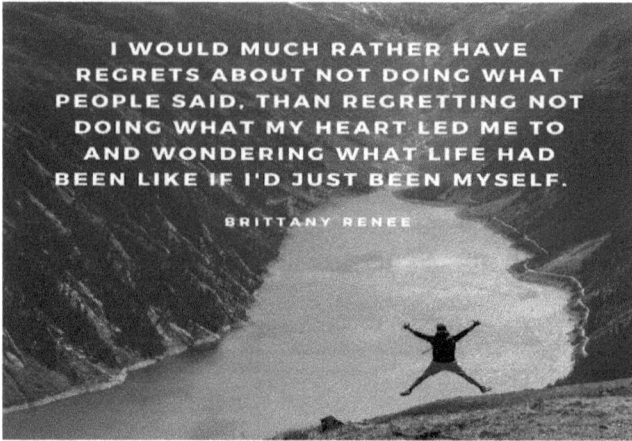

I WOULD MUCH RATHER HAVE REGRETS ABOUT NOT DOING WHAT PEOPLE SAID, THAN REGRETTING NOT DOING WHAT MY HEART LED ME TO AND WONDERING WHAT LIFE HAD BEEN LIKE IF I'D JUST BEEN MYSELF.

BRITTANY RENEE

It's much easier to follow in someone else's footsteps. Believing in your heart and making your own choices can be daunting at times, but it's an important part of the learning process. Mistakes are teachers, and victories are windfalls.

You will experience true celebration if you live your life through your own heart and mind. Being yourself allows you to grow. Being someone else only brings regret.

- Determine if you are doing what is right for you.
- Ask yourself, "If I do this, can I (will I?) pat myself on the back when it is completed?"
- Allow yourself to be who you are, rather than what others think you should be.

Self-Reflection Questions:

1. What prevents me from holding my head up high and congratulating myself for the things I accomplish?

2. Did I do this because I wanted to, or because someone else wanted me to do it?

3. Do I make choices that are right for me, or to make myself something I'm not?

At the end of this week of reflection:

- This last week's quote and tips were relevant in my life because:

- My reflections last week resulted in me understanding:

- The benefits I will receive by applying my understanding are:

WEEK 28

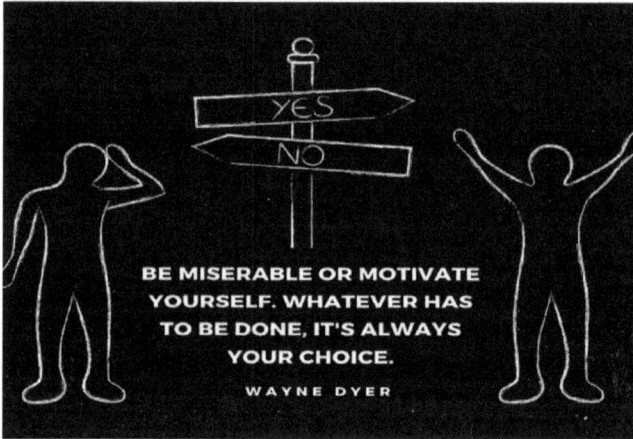

The choice is always yours to move ahead or fall behind. Allowing yourself to drown in your own misery is an easy way out.

Finding the motivation to pick yourself up, create a better life, and move on takes determination. In the end, your life is what you want it to be.

- Determine if you're miserable or motivated.
- If you feel unhappiness about anything, ask yourself if you chose to be that way.
- Find the motivational tools to help you through your life's journey.

Self-Reflection Questions:

1. Why am I not satisfied with my life the way it is? What keeps me from being satisfied with my life?

2. How can I motivate myself to improve my life?

3. What choices will I make to better my life?

At the end of this week of reflection:

- This last week's quote and tips were relevant in my life because:

- My reflections last week resulted in me understanding:

- The benefits I will receive by applying my understanding are:

WEEK 29

IT'S KIND OF FUN
TO DO THE
IMPOSSIBLE.

WALT DISNEY

"That's impossible and can't be done." Really? How will you know if you do not try? Almost anything is possible ... if you set your mind to it. Not only is it possible, but it can be fun and exciting to make it happen.

When you look at the world around you, don't most things seem impossible when you first start out? But, if you have the vision, and work to make it come true, it often does!

- Look at the situation and determine the pros and cons of why you think it is impossible.
- Imagine what it would be like if you accomplished what you thought was the impossible!
- Take it step-by-step and persevere until you succeed.

Self-Reflection Questions:

1. Why do I believe this is impossible?

2. What would make this impossible task achievable?

3. How can I find the positive outcomes in everything I do?

At the end of this week of reflection:

- This last week's quote and tips were relevant in my life because:

- My reflections last week resulted in me understanding:

- The benefits I will receive by applying my understanding are:

WEEK 30

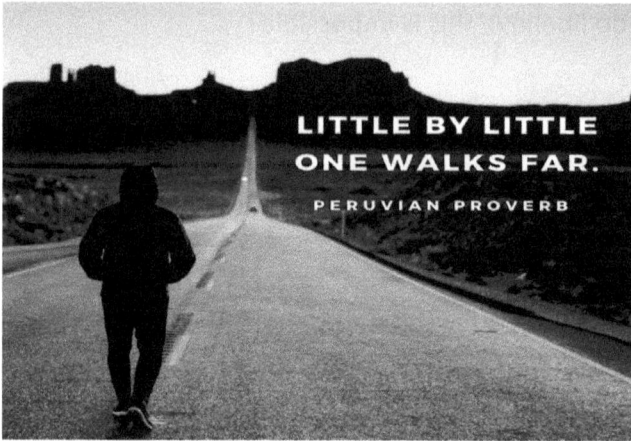

LITTLE BY LITTLE
ONE WALKS FAR.

PERUVIAN PROVERB

How do you get through life? By taking baby steps and learning as you go. It is the little things in life that carry you forward. One step at a time, you grow from your life.

From the minute you are born, it is the small accomplishments that keep you moving forward on your journey. These tasks may be explained to you, demonstrated and taught to you, and you practice them before you excel in them. As you accomplish the little achievements, you realize the small successes lead to greater achievements.

- Determine your starting point and work your way up.
- Determine what action steps you can take to move you forward.
- Realize you can go far by taking things one step at a time.

Self-Reflection Questions:

1. How have I congratulated myself on my small successes?

2. Why don't I understand that all my goals can't be accomplished in a day?

3. What large goals can I breakdown into smaller action steps?

At the end of this week of reflection:

- This last week's quote and tips were relevant in my life because:

- My reflections last week resulted in me understanding:

- The benefits I will receive by applying my understanding are:

WEEK 31

TO MOVE AHEAD YOU NEED TO BELIEVE IN YOURSELF, HAVE CONVICTION IN YOUR BELIEFS AND THE CONFIDENCE TO EXECUTE THOSE BELIEFS.

ADLIN SINCLAIR

As you go through life, one of your biggest chores is to learn to believe in yourself. You must build your confidence and trust your beliefs.

To move ahead, you must have strong beliefs and be willing to stand by them.

- Take a long look at who you really are and what you believe in.
- Determine how to firmly stand behind those beliefs.
- Find ways to use those beliefs to move ahead in your life.

Self-Reflection Questions:

1. Why do I really believe in myself with all my heart and soul?

2. Describe what it takes to stand behind my belief?

3. How do I stay confident to stand up for my beliefs even when faced with opposition?

At the end of this week of reflection:

- This last week's quote and tips were relevant in my life because:

- My reflections last week resulted in me understanding:

- The benefits I will receive by applying my understanding are:

WEEK 32

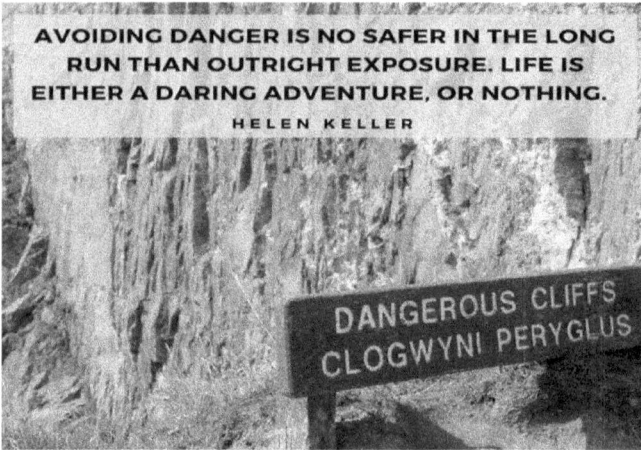

AVOIDING DANGER IS NO SAFER IN THE LONG RUN THAN OUTRIGHT EXPOSURE. LIFE IS EITHER A DARING ADVENTURE, OR NOTHING.

HELEN KELLER

DANGEROUS CLIFFS
CLOGWYNI PERYGLUS

On your life's journey, you find yourself in situations where you want to hide instead of taking chances and/or face the challenges and consequences to get ahead. You must successfully deal with fear to take chances.

From the moment you are born, to the day you take your last breath, those opportunities are everywhere. If you decide to never take a chance, life would never be filled with adventure; there would be no learning, and in the end, there would be nothing in your life but missed opportunities.

- Make a list of a few opportunities you've allowed to pass by.
- List the reasons you were afraid to try these opportunities.
- Look within yourself to find your strength to chase the adventure.

Self-Reflection Questions:

1. How might my life be worse off by not taking chances?

2. What might I learn if I took this chance?

3. How would my life be richer if I would just try?

At the end of this week of reflection:

- This last week's quote and tips were relevant in my life because:

- My reflections last week resulted in me understanding:

- The benefits I will receive by applying my understanding are:

WEEK 33

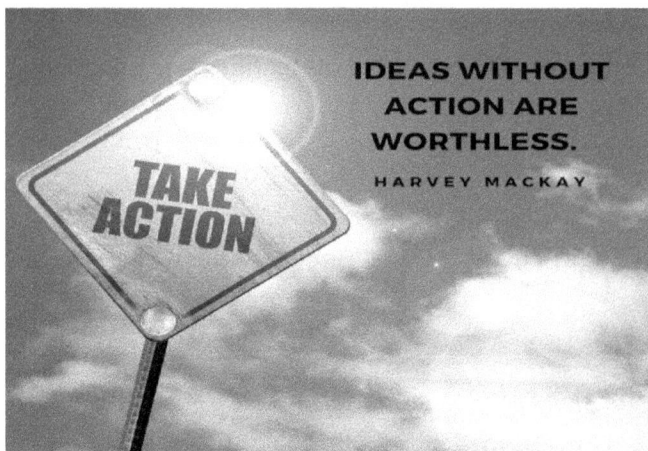

Great ideas come to everyone. The ideas sound good, but perhaps you think the idea is overwhelming or unreachable. Your ideas remain a dream and drain your energy when you don't put them into action.

Actions are an important part of your life. To enhance your life and live it to the fullest, you must take your ideas and take the action necessary to make those ideas become a reality.

- Write down your ideas.
- Investigate what it takes to make your idea become a reality.
- Take the time to work through your ideas and the steps necessary to bring them to fruition.

Self-Reflection Questions:

1. What would it take to make MY idea a reality?

2. What is stopping me from putting this idea into action?

3. What things could I accomplish by making my idea a reality?

At the end of this week of reflection:

- This last week's quote and tips were relevant in my life because:

- My reflections last week resulted in me understanding:

- The benefits I will receive by applying my understanding are:

WEEK 34

FOCUS ON THE JOURNEY, NOT THE DESTINATION. JOY IS FOUND NOT IN FINISHING AN ACTIVITY BUT IN DOING IT.

GREG ANDERSON

When you look at your life, you must agree it is a journey with a final destination. If you spend your life focusing only on where you will end up, the journey is for nothing.

To be truly happy in your life you must focus on where your life is at the moment. Each day is new and exciting. Living each day to the fullest is where you can find the joy of living. Take the time to enjoy life's journey ... day-by-day.

- Look around you; where has your life's journey taken you?
- Dig deep inside to find the joy in the everyday things you do.
- Pat yourself on the back for even your smallest accomplishments in your journey.

Self-Reflection Questions:

1. What are those things I can pinpoint and describe?

2. Where can I slow down to pace myself towards my goal(s)?

3. Where does my focus lie as I take this journey through my life?

At the end of this week of reflection:

- This last week's quote and tips were relevant in my life because:

- My reflections last week resulted in me understanding:

- The benefits I will receive by applying my understanding are:

WEEK 35

THE AMOUNT OF GOOD LUCK COMING YOUR WAY DEPENDS ON YOUR WILLINGNESS TO ACT.

BARBARA SHER

How many times have you heard yourself say "If it wasn't for bad luck I would have no luck at all?" It could be too often. The good luck in your life comes from within … not from others.

When it comes to luck, you must take action and work at bringing good things into your life. By taking action, you determine where your life goes, what things are parts of your life, and the good coming your way … because of the choices you've made.

- Make a list of the good things you feel you have missed.
- Ask yourself "Do I wait on someone else to make life happen?"
- Decide if you have the willingness to act.

Self-Reflection Questions:

1. How is depending solely on others instead of acting myself negatively impacting my life ?

2. What are the resources I need to create opportunities in my life?

3. How will I take responsibility for my own good luck?

At the end of this week of reflection:

- This last week's quote and tips were relevant in my life because:

- My reflections last week resulted in me understanding:

- The benefits I will receive by applying my understanding are:

WEEK 36

WE MUST FIRST THINK "I CAN," THEN BEHAVE APPROPRIATELY ALONG THAT LINE OF THOUGHT.

MARSHA SINETAR

Remember the story of the little train that could? You can fall short in believing you can. It is amazing what you can accomplish when you believe in yourself! Believing in your own abilities comes with practice and the urge to learn.

Knowing in your heart and mind that you can do something, and follow through to show yourself you can, is an important part of being able to build the life you desire.

- Tell yourself you can do anything if you set your mind to it.
- Choose a challenge, believe you can do it, and follow that challenge through to fruition.
- Work on the little things first to pave your way to the bigger accomplishments.

Self-Reflection Questions:

1. What or who is stopping me from believing in myself?

2. How can I eliminate the procrastination and start proactively moving past the doubt?

3. What are those steps and how often do I exercise those positive steps towards small and large goals in my life?

At the end of this week of reflection:

- This last week's quote and tips were relevant in my life because:

- My reflections last week resulted in me understanding:

- The benefits I will receive by applying my understanding are:

WEEK 37

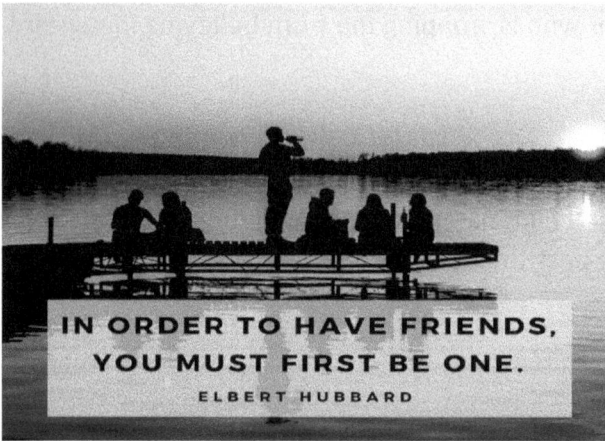

IN ORDER TO HAVE FRIENDS,
YOU MUST FIRST BE ONE.
ELBERT HUBBARD

Some folks in your life you consider acquaintances, and others you consider friends. How many of these friends are your true friends?

To have a true friend you must first be a true friend. Loving and caring brings out your good qualities. These qualities can then be passed on to others in a friendship that can last a lifetime.

- Look deep within yourself to find the qualities you like about yourself.
- Ask yourself if these qualities would make you a true friend.
- Look at the reasons you would consider others to be your true friend.

Self-Reflection Questions:

1. Who are my 'true' friends? What acquaintances could become true friends?

2. What do I offer unequivocally to my true friends with no expectations of return of the same?

3. How can I support my friends when they need me?

At the end of this week of reflection:

- This last week's quote and tips were relevant in my life because:

- My reflections last week resulted in me understanding:

- The benefits I will receive by applying my understanding are:

WEEK 38

LEAP, AND THE NET WILL APPEAR.

JULIE CAMERON

Taking that leap is a scary venture. Are you afraid of falling on the ground and smacking your face? These leaps (or falls or both) are how you learn and grow.

Something good comes out of everything. If you are afraid to leap, you'll never know. Life is a chance. Without realizing it, you take chances each day without harm. Why? Because there is a net and you know the safety is there at the right moments.

- You can begin with small leaps.
- Talk to yourself about the good that comes from taking these leaps.
- Look at the chances you take each day and ask yourself what nets appear to keep you from falling.

Self-Reflection Questions:

1. What holds me back from taking the leap?

2. Will the rewards, or a possible bump on the head, be worth the risk? What risks are there? What are the rewards?

3. What safety nets will be there to catch me when I leap? If I take the leap I have been scared to take, what safety net could or should I put in place?

At the end of this week of reflection:

- This last week's quote and tips were relevant in my life because:

- My reflections last week resulted in me understanding:

- The benefits I will receive by applying my understanding are:

WEEK 39

THE FUTURE IS PURCHASED
BY THE PRESENT.

SAMUEL JOHNSON

What you do in your life today will always affect your life in the future. Your actions – each and every day – sets the destination for your life.

Although you may not want to dwell on it, you must realize everything you do will have a consequence. Making the best of each day will set a precedence for the best yet to come!

- Look at what you do daily that may affect your future.
- Determine how the good things in your life bring an even better future.
- Make a list of the things you need to change to begin to build the future you want.

Self-Reflection Questions:

1. How do the actions I take in the present affect my future – in a positive or negative way?

2. What have I done in my past that affected my life and the future I see before me? Have I made some bad decisions to please others or have decisions been selfish to deprive others, and I suffered the consequences?

3. How can I change my present to ensure I have the future I hope for? Mentally, physically, emotionally?

At the end of this week of reflection:

- This last week's quote and tips were relevant in my life because:

- My reflections last week resulted in me understanding:

- The benefits I will receive by applying my understanding are:

WEEK 40

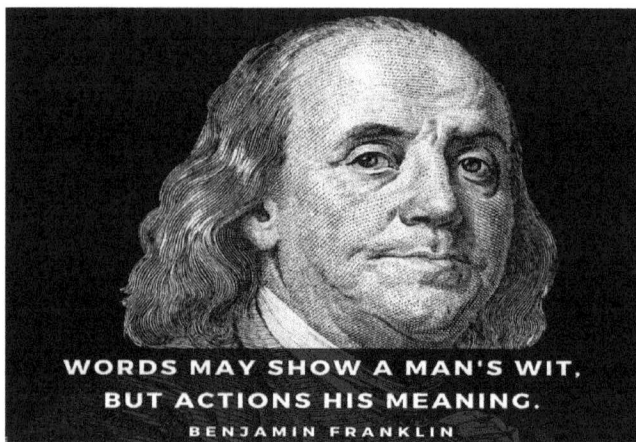

WORDS MAY SHOW A MAN'S WIT,
BUT ACTIONS HIS MEANING.
BENJAMIN FRANKLIN

Actions always speak louder than words. What you do shows your true being. Your every-day actions, from the moment you wake up in the morning until you lay your head down to sleep at night, shows everyone who you really are.

To be believed and trusted you must not only say the words, but also show the actions. A word is only as good as the action that comes with the spoken or written word?

- Take the time to listen to what you say.
- Act upon your words as if your life depended on it.
- Never make a promise that you don't intend to keep.

Self-Reflection Questions:

1. How often do I listen to others only to formulate a response, then regret what I say to others?

2. What was the impact when you promised to do something for someone and did not follow through?

3. How do I feel when someone tells me something and then acts the exact opposite?

At the end of this week of reflection:

- This last week's quote and tips were relevant in my life because:

- My reflections last week resulted in me understanding:

- The benefits I will receive by applying my understanding are:

WEEK 41

SKILLS TO DO COMES OF DOING.

RALPH WALDO EMERSON

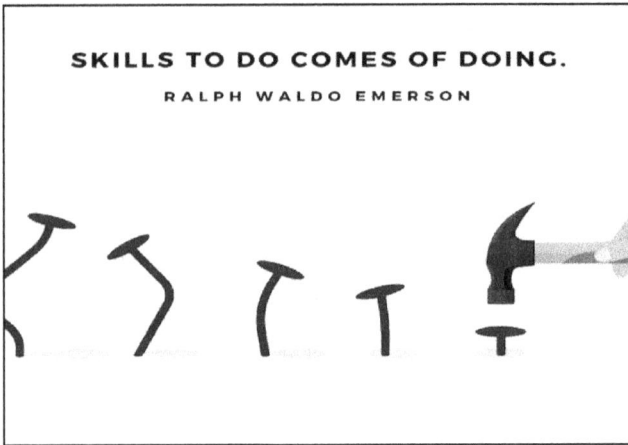

There's no truer phrase than "practice makes perfect." Life's skills are easy to learn, but hard to perfect. The only way you can perfect these skills is by repeating them.

Skills, such as conversational dialogue, are learned early and perfected over years of interaction with family, then friends, and peers. Other skills are taught through family environment and social learning, as well as through formal schooling. You continue to practice for your entire life. The best way to learn is by doing.

- Make a list of the skills you'd like to master.
- Determine how long you must practice them each day to master them.
- Follow through with practicing them every day.

Self-Reflection Questions:

1. Who has told me I lack skills, or finesse in a certain skill? Why have they shared that information with me?

2. What actions do I want to take to continually develop my skills?

3. How can I schedule time in my everyday life to perfect skills that I need to get ahead in my goals and objectives?

At the end of this week of reflection:

- This last week's quote and tips were relevant in my life because:

- My reflections last week resulted in me understanding:

- The benefits I will receive by applying my understanding are:

WEEK 42

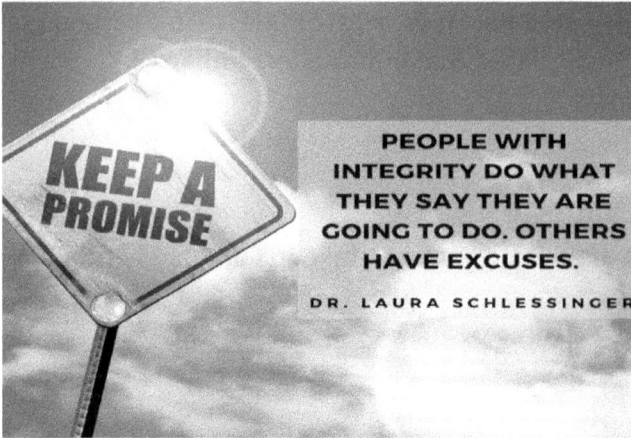

An excuse can be an easy way out. Whether you have made a promise to yourself or someone else, creating an excuse to get out of it is easy. Even a bad excuse seems better than no excuse.

When you say you're going to do something, do it. If you cannot or do not want to do something you are asked to do, do not be ashamed to say no.

People believe in what you say you will do; being honest and admitting you cannot do it is better than committing and then not following through.

- Know what you realistically can and can't do.
- Be sincere in your promises.
- Follow through.

Self-Reflection Questions:

1. How often do you make a promise to someone and never follow-through?

2. Why do I sometimes not follow through on my promises?

3. Why is being honesty with others more powerful than making excuses for not being able to keep a promise?

At the end of this week of reflection:

- This last week's quote and tips were relevant in my life because:

- My reflections last week resulted in me understanding:

- The benefits I will receive by applying my understanding are:

WEEK 43

> **THERE ARE COSTS AND RISKS TO A PROGRAM OF ACTION, BUT THEY ARE FAR LESS THAN THE LONG-RANGE RISKS AND COSTS OF COMFORTABLE INACTION.**
>
> JOHN F. KENNEDY

John F. Kennedy Space Cente

Taking action, whether it is starting a business or cooking breakfast, will have a price. This price may be good, or it may be costly, but at least you'll know because you did it.

Sitting on your hands and not acting has long-term risks and can cost plenty. Have you ever passed up a chance at something, only to regret it later? Every action has its risks, yes, but not acting can sometimes cost even more.

- Don't be afraid to try.
- Start with small actions and work your way up to the bigger ones.
- Decide if being comfortable is more important than learning and living.

Self-Reflection Questions:

1. Pick something you have decided not to do in the past and explain why you shied away from doing it?

2. Name some actions you did follow-though on in the past that resulted in a positive feeling of accomplishment?

3. Am I simply lazy or am I scared of something?

At the end of this week of reflection:

• This last week's quote and tips were relevant in my life because:

• My reflections last week resulted in me understanding:

• The benefits I will receive by applying my understanding are:

WEEK 44

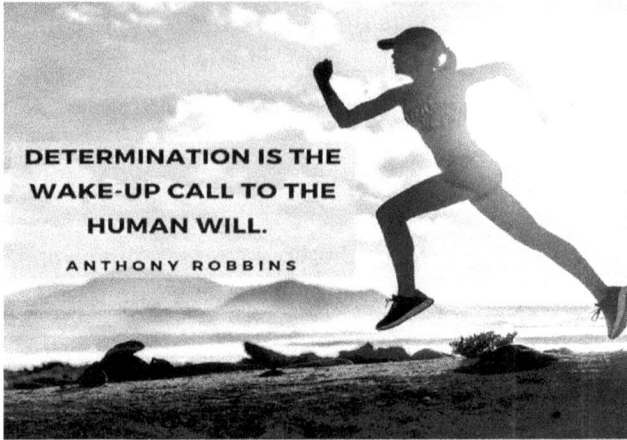

DETERMINATION IS THE
WAKE-UP CALL TO THE
HUMAN WILL.

ANTHONY ROBBINS

Most of us have a will to succeed. This 'will' is set in our psyche by our determination to reach our goals and fulfill our dreams. Determination is a necessary part of life's success. If we're not determined to achieve and succeed, our lives will always remain the same.

Determination gets you up in the morning, helps you make it through your day, and gets you to sleep at night. Determination lets you fight your battles and puts you on the path to learn new skills. As a human, you will continue to grow when you are determined.

- Don't give up.
- Dig down deep within yourself to find the determination hidden within.
- Know that the more determined you are the better chance you have to succeed.

Self-Reflection Questions:

1. Did I give up on something without really even trying? What was that and why didn't I want to try at the time? Was my plate full or was I scared to try and fail?

2. If I had been more determined to succeed, would I have accomplished my goal? What did I need then to push harder to take on that project and succeed, and what do I need now to accept the next accomplishment and goal to succeed?

3. Do I have the will-power it takes to persist until my tasks are completed? If I don't have the will-power, how can I develop it or get it? What do I need (tools, empowerment, support) to develop that will-power?

At the end of this week of reflection:

- This last week's quote and tips were relevant in my life because:

- My reflections last week resulted in me understanding:

- The benefits I will receive by applying my understanding are:

WEEK 45

DREAM AS IF YOU'LL LIVE FOREVER. LIVE AS IF YOU WILL DIE TOMORROW.

JAMES DEAN

Dreamers know that when you dream … you must dream big … and extend those dreams into the future. Dreams give us hope for today and every day of our lives. If you only dream, but do not strive to make those dreams come true, you never truly live!

Dream for the future, but live for the day. Enjoy your life; strive each day to make your dreams come true and find your true hopes in life fulfilled.

- Enjoy each moment you live.
- Take advantage of opportunities now; don't put off action until tomorrow.
- Take the time to dream the impossible dream.

Self-Reflection Questions:

1. What gets my funny-bone tingling? Who am I around that makes me laugh?

2. What do I do daily that brings me pleasure in my life?

3. Am I scared to succeed because that will bring on more responsibilities?

At the end of this week of reflection:

- This last week's quote and tips were relevant in my life because:

- My reflections last week resulted in me understanding:

- The benefits I will receive by applying my understanding are:

WEEK 46

THE MOST IMPORTANT THING ABOUT GOALS IS HAVING ONE.

GEOFFRY F. ABERT

Everyone must have something in their life to strive for and be proud of. People go through life never trying to achieve a single goal. Setting goals is part of growing and achieving them brings you fulfillment.

Even the smallest goal, such as getting out of bed at a certain time each morning, or a larger goal that might include starting your own business can be an accomplishment. The first step is the act of creating the goal. Once you have a goal in place, plan the steps, take the steps, and repeat the process to achieve your desires.

- Make a list of things you'd like to achieve in your life.
- Start with short term goals to show yourself how easy they are to set and accomplish.
- Take a chance and set a long-term goal; then take the steps to make it a reality.

Self-Reflection Questions:

1. Name some short-term, and long-term, goals that I have considered, then followed through on.

2. What goals have set, but never made a plan to reach them? (e.g., I want to be a millionaire, but never got a job or built a business to make it happen?)

3. Do you accomplish more short-term goals that really are not connected to long-term goals, or are you repeating the same short-term goals with no end in sight?

At the end of this week of reflection:

- This last week's quote and tips were relevant in my life because:

- My reflections last week resulted in me understanding:

- The benefits I will receive by applying my understanding are:

WEEK 47

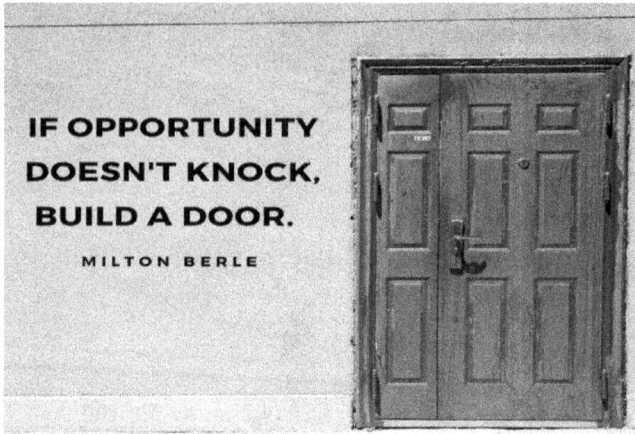

IF OPPORTUNITY
DOESN'T KNOCK,
BUILD A DOOR.

MILTON BERLE

People will sit back and wait for an opportunity to present itself. Waiting for opportunities is like fishing without bait.

Recognizing opportunities when they do show up, as well as, creating your own opportunities are the best ways to achieve success. Opportunities find you, the moment you give yourself the chance and remain open to the possibilities.

- Don't wait for someone else to find opportunities for you.
- Recognize opportunities and act promptly.
- Create a list of things you want to accomplish and determine what opportunities are available to help you achieve your goals.

Self-Reflection Questions:

1. What doors can I open to find the opportunity I've been waiting for? What are my goals? What needs to happen to reach those goals. Where can I create my own opportunities (.e.g., creating a meeting with someone) to accomplish those identified goals?

2. Will I feel a sense of accomplishment if I take this chance? How will that accomplishment make me feel? What will my family, friends, and peers feel about me when I achieve that goal?

3. Am I afraid this opportunity won't work out? Why? Will inaction bring better results?

At the end of this week of reflection:

- This last week's quote and tips were relevant in my life because:

- My reflections last week resulted in me understanding:

- The benefits I will receive by applying my understanding are:

WEEK 48

THE DICTIONARY IS THE ONLY PLACE WHERE SUCCESS COMES BEFORE WORK.

MARK TWAIN

suc·cess (sək·ses′) *n*
something attempted
etc. 3. Attainment
suc·cess·ful (sək·ses

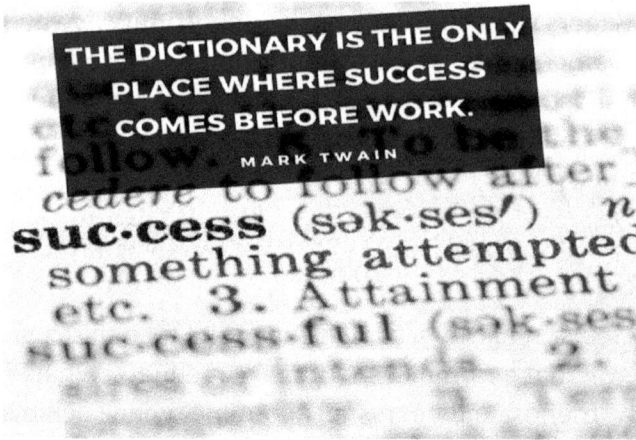

Success doesn't just happen. To achieve your goals and live the life you desire, you must determine the steps that will get you there.

Do the work first and then you'll see success. Just like the farmer, you must prepare the soil, plant the seeds, water the plants, and pull the weeds to reap the harvest.

- Look at the successes you've achieved.
- List the work you accomplished that led to success.
- List the work you can do to achieve your current goals, and then follow through.

Self-Reflection Questions:

1. List a few successes and what you did to make them happen?

2. To achieve success, who can I talk to for assistance? What needs to happen in baby-steps? What do I need to invest in myself to do to get there?

3. How will I stay motivated for my future success?   Do I set my mind-set daily for a positive attitude? Do I laugh daily to keep a positive mood?

At the end of this week of reflection:

- This last week's quote and tips were relevant in my life because:

- My reflections last week resulted in me understanding:

- The benefits I will receive by applying my understanding are:

WEEK 49

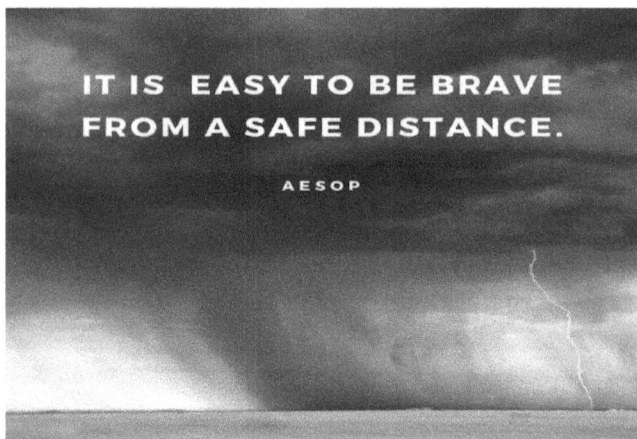

IT IS EASY TO BE BRAVE
FROM A SAFE DISTANCE.

AESOP

It's much easier to be steadfast if you're not facing danger. Yet when you do this – avoiding risk, you don't learn and grow from those challenges. When you stay where it is safe, you stagnate.

Facing your problems and being brave enough to do what is necessary to conquer those challenging problems will help you build the strength, confidence, and knowledge to succeed.

- Determine the reality of your problem.
- Look within for the courage to face your problems head-on.
- Remember by facing your problems you become a stronger person and pave the way for being able to meet future challenges successfully.

Self-Reflection Questions:

1. What makes me afraid to face my problems? Have you been taught or have a mentor model the fear of resolving issues?

2. What can I do to have the courage to tackle this problem with an open mind? Do I need to be physically bigger, mentally more resolved, or psychologically more jazzed?

3. How has playing it safe caused me to be disappointed in myself?

At the end of this week of reflection:

- This last week's quote and tips were relevant in my life because:

- My reflections last week resulted in me understanding:

- The benefits I will receive by applying my understanding are:

WEEK 50

OUR GREATEST BATTLES ARE
THAT WITH OUR OWN MINDS.
JAMESON FRANK

Your mind may be in a whirlwind, and you don't know which way to go. Being able to think constructively with a clear mind and a level head is the best way to win the battles in your life.

Stress reduction techniques, like meditation, yoga, exercise, and keeping an open mind can give you tools to sustain inner peace. This sense of calm will enable you to think things through with clarity and confidence, so you don't fight battles in your mind.

- Keep an open mind no matter what your struggle might be.
- Listen to yourself and what your mind is saying to you.
- Know you can take control of your thoughts by separating facts from stories.

Self-Reflection Questions:

1. What current issue are you struggling over that you have not yet looked at the pros and cons from both perspectives (yours and the other person's)? What are the facts? What are assumptions or non-truths?

2. How can I control my mind wandering off in different directions? How can I curtail my emotions from taking over my logical thinking about a problem?

3. What methods and techniques can I use to get the emotions and thoughts under control for more positive and logical decision-making?

At the end of this week of reflection:

- This last week's quote and tips were relevant in my life because:

- My reflections last week resulted in me understanding:

- The benefits I will receive by applying my understanding are:

WEEK 51

PERSEVERANCE IS FALLING NINETEEN TIMES AND SUCCEEDING THE TWENTIETH.

JULIE ANDREWS

Perseverance keeps your mind and body going. It is easy to quit when you fail. It might be the first time you try or the 10th time, but don't just give up when you should keep trying.

Never give up! There's always a way and perseverance will keep you going until you find that way. Perseverance will make you strong, give you courage, and show you that you're a winner.

- Remember it's better to succeed than never to have tried at all.
- Failure is only a state of mind while succeeding is a state of euphoria.
- Allow yourself the patience to continue until you beat the odds.

Self-Reflection Questions:

1. Name some instances where I have quit when I should have keep going. What is cost, work, other's opinions that caused me to make that negative decision?

2. What are my goals, and do I daily remind myself of the future with the goal achieved?

3. Life is hard. Sometimes one loses control over circumstances. What can I do to obtain the control over my own impatience?

At the end of this week of reflection:

- This last week's quote and tips were relevant in my life because:

- My reflections last week resulted in me understanding:

- The benefits I will receive by applying my understanding are:

WEEK 52

> ## "I CAN'T DO IT" NEVER ACCOMPLISHED ANYTHING; "I WILL TRY" HAS PERFORMED WONDERS.
>
> ### GEORGE P. BURNHAM
>
> *Try try again*

If you decide you can't do something, then you will not accomplish it. Telling yourself you will try gives you incentive to look at the situation, not give up, and eventually succeed.

If you have enough faith in yourself to at least try, then you give yourself an opportunity to pat yourself on the back, whether you succeed or not. Trying to achieve a goal will help you build wisdom and will power to continue at every chance.

- Look at the situation and ask yourself why you think you can't do it.
- List the reasons why you should try.
- Realize it's much more rewarding to try than to say, "I can't."

Self-Reflection Questions:

1. Looking back, what have I allowed to interfere with my ability to establish direction and set goals?

2. Name a time I stopped trying and regretted my decision? How will I prevent not trying from happening again?

3. How did I learn and grow from a difficult task I accomplished?

At the end of this week of reflection:

- This last week's quote and tips were relevant in my life because:

- My reflections last week resulted in me understanding:

- The benefits I will receive by applying my understanding are:

ABOUT THE AUTHOR

Like you, John Bentley has experienced the ups and downs of life. One moment you are on 'cloud nine,' and at other times you may become confused and not quite sure of where to turn next. Through it all John has come to understand that leading yourself is the key to staying motivated, overcoming challenges, and solving the problems that will occur in your life.

John's 'aha moment' came early in his Air Force career when he received feedback that his leadership style under pressure was similar to someone opening a coke can after it was shaken. This led him on a journey to discover why he behaved poorly in tough situations. The findings John uncovered were not easy to accept. But, he possessed the desire to learn and willingness to overcome limiting beliefs that caused him to struggle, be frustrated, and limit his opportunities for success. His inner journey provided him with peace and the motivational answers to his current success.

After he retired from the Air Force, John founded *Power 2 Transform*. Since 2003, his sole focus is on helping people master the art of self-leadership, especially when faced with adversity. His goals, whether speaking, coaching, or training are always the same – equipping people to leverage their strengths and mitigate their limitations – so they can be more effective for themselves and others.

POWER 2 TRANSFORM SERVICES

- Keynote Speaker
- Conference Breakout Session Presenter
- Leadership and Team Development
  - ✓ Half-Day Seminars
  - ✓ Full-Day Workshops
- Coaching Opportunities

Contact John at:

john@power2transform.com

For more information visit:

www.power2transform.com

www.linkedin.com/in/power2transform

www.twitter.com/power2transform

http://www.facebook.com/power2transformnow/

ABOUT THE BOOK

Time to learn, change, and grow is at a valuable premium. Have you ever lit a match-stick and thought, "Why wasn't the match-stick burning before I rubbed it against the box?" Motivation that one seeks externally is already inside us. Think back to songs you love, books you have read, and the discoveries you have witnessed – the motivations these inspired were already inside your brain – long before you encountered them. Think of yourself as a matchstick and quotes are the striker. Whenever we rub ourselves against a quote, we 'light a fire' or motivate ourselves.

The appeal for quotes seem to lie in a combination of appropriate wordsmithing, motivational psychology, and a measure of self-selection. People who tend to feel inspired by motivational quotes are going to find them more resonant to their lives and situations. This book will create the opportunity for you to focus on yourself and creating a more valuable, fulfilling, and satisfying life. You have the right tool in your hand if you are ready to transform your negative thinking into a positive mindset by applying practical tips to grow into your best self!

This book will ...

- ... provide you practical ideas and inspiring quotes to stay motivated despite your current circumstances.
- ... help guide you to knowledge, there is more to life; thought-provoking tips help you get started 'self-motivating'.
- ... enable you to find and create faster, better ideas to become mentally healthier, emotionally happier, and to guide you to a successful life.
- ... help you stop procrastinating and to motivate you to achieve real results for your life.
- ... enable you to take action and to develop and achieve the personal goals you've always dreamed about.

www.ingramcontent.com/pod-product-compliance
Lightning Source LLC
Chambersburg PA
CBHW070519030426
42337CB00016B/2027